How to Draw
Flowers and Trees

For Jesse, Jasmine, Justin, Jordan, Melina, and Matthew

Published in the United States of America by The Child's World®
PO Box 326 • Chanhassen, MN 55317-0326
800-599-READ • www.childsworld.com

Acknowledgments
Illustration and Design: Rob Court
Production: The Creative Spark, San Juan Capistrano, CA

Registration
The Child's World® and associated logo is the sole property and registered
trademark of The Child's World®.
The Scribbles Institute™, Young Artist Basics, and their associated logos are
the sole property and registered trademarks of The Scribbles Institute™.

Library of Congress Cataloging-in-Publication Data
Court, Rob, 1956–
  How to draw flowers and trees / by Rob Court.
    p. cm. — (Doodle books)
  ISBN-13: 978-1-59296-807-7 (library bound : alk. paper)
  ISBN-10: 1-59296-807-4 (library bound : alk. paper)
  1. Flowers in art—Juvenile literature. 2. Trees in art—Juvenile literature.
  3. Drawing—Technique—Juvenile literature. I. Title.

NC805.C68 2007
743'.73—dc22
                                          2006031561

The Scribbles Institute™

How to Draw

Flowers and Trees

by Rob Court

The Child's World®

dandelion

1

2

3

4

tulip

1

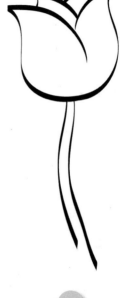

2

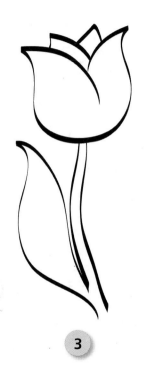

3

4

palm tree

1

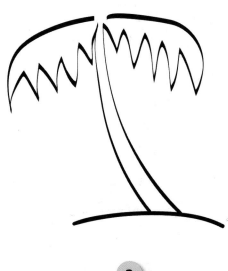

2

3

4

oak leaf

1

2

3

4

oak tree

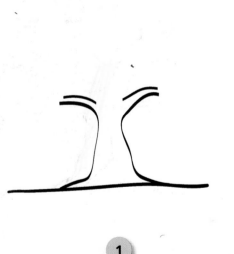

1

2

3

4

daisy

1

2

3

4

3

4

orange tree

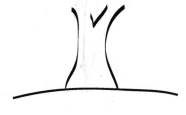

1

2

3

4

willow tree

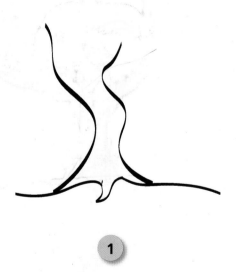

1

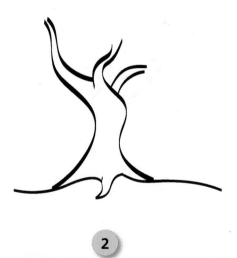

2

3

4

ivy

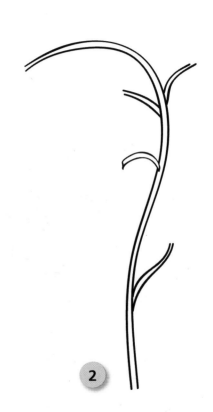

3

4

1

2

3

4

1

2

3

4

sunflower

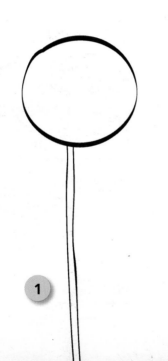

1

2

3

4

tree house

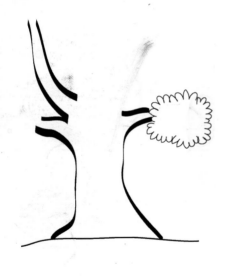

1

2

3

4

lines

 horizontal

vertical

 angled

curved

 thick

thin

  point

dotted

squiggly

dashed

loop

Move a point to make a line.

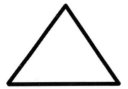 Connect lines to make a shape.

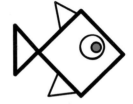 Shapes make all kinds of wonderful things!

Repeating dots, lines, and shapes makes patterns.

About the Author

Rob Court is a graphic artist and illustrator. He started the Scribbles Institute to help students, parents, and teachers learn about drawing and visual art. Please visit www.scribblesinstitute.com